THE
FORGOTTEN TRIBES
OF CHINA

THE
FORGOTTEN TRIBES
OF CHINA

KEVIN SINCLAIR

photographs by
PAUL LAU

additional photographs by
Geoff Bartram, Mike Langford, Rebecca Lee,
Leong Ka Tai, Paul Ricketts, Jan Whiting Subiaco

MEREHURST PRESS
LONDON

LEONG KA TAI

Page 1: A fiery mask from the farmers' opera of the Bouyei minority in Guizhou.
Page 2: The red braids signify the clan of this Tibetan nomad.
Endpapers: People of the Miao minority in Guangxi Province carrying their goods to sell in the third of March Festival market. Photo: Paul Lau.

Produced by
Intercontinental Publishing Corporation Limited
4th Floor, 69 Wyndham Street, Central Hong Kong
Telex 83499 PPA HX; Fax 5-8101683
A member of the Weldon-Hardie Group of Companies
Sydney   Auckland   Hong Kong   London   Chicago

Published in Great Britain by

Merehurst Press
5 Great James Street
London WC1N 3DA

ISBN 0 948075 67 8

Editorial director: Elaine Russell
Project coordinator: Sheena Coupe
Editor: Annabel Beams
Index: Dianne Regtop
Picture research: Mary-Dawn Earley
Map: Steven Dunbar
Designer: Warren Penney
Production: Kate Smyth, Sue Tickner

Typeset by Amazing Faces, Sydney, Australia
Colour separations by Universal Colour Scanning Ltd,
Hong Kong
Printed by Everbest Printing Co Ltd, Hong Kong
Printed in Hong Kong

A KEVIN WELDON PRODUCTION

CONTENTS

Mongol
Mongol
Kazak
Mongol
Uygur
Uygur Han
Uygur Han
Uygur
Mongol Han
Kazak
Kazak Han
Hui
Han
H
Tibetan
Tibetan
Yi
Yi
Bai
Bou
Dai
Zhuang
Bou
Yi
Hani
Yao
Dai

CHINA'S PEOPLE

A mosaic of cultures

The map shows, in a generalised and simplified way, the distribution
of the Chinese people, including the Han majority. It cannot indicate
the complexities of all minority groupings, nor the extent of overlap
between various peoples. The major language families of China are
distinguished by colour; within these language families, the most
numerous peoples are indicated by type.

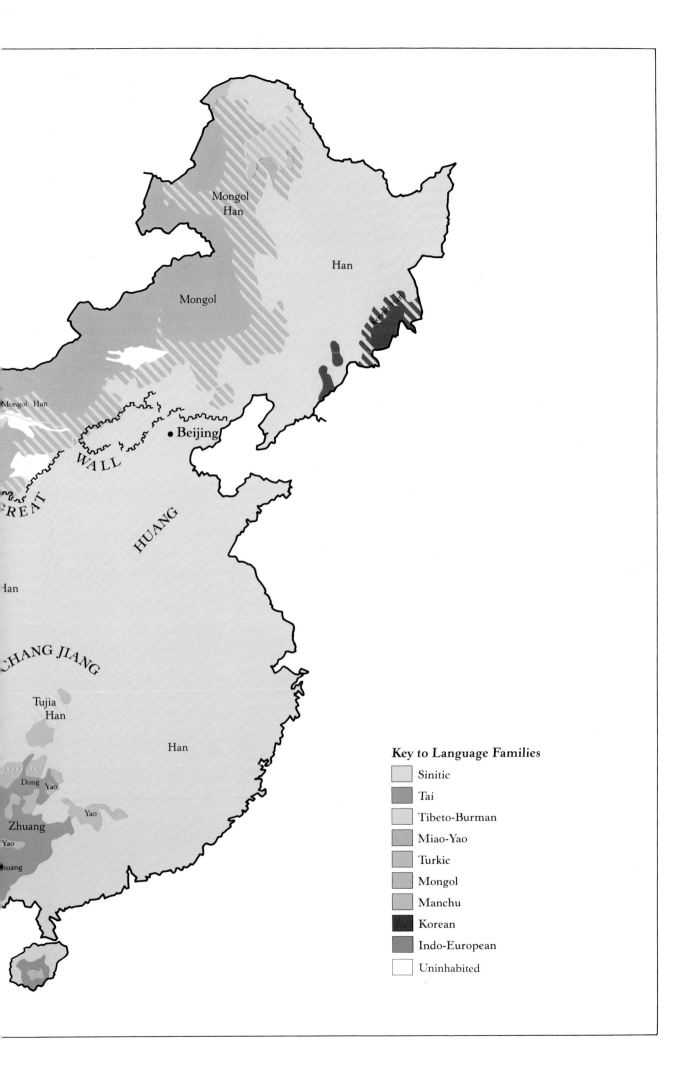

Mongol
Han

Han

Mongol

Korean Han

Mongol Han

● Beijing

WALL

GREAT

HUANG

Han

CHANG JIANG

Tujia
Han

Han

Dong Yao

Yao

Zhuang

Yao

Zhuang

Key to Language Families

Sinitic

Tai

Tibeto-Burman

Miao-Yao

Turkic

Mongol

Manchu

Korean

Indo-European

Uninhabited

THE TWO CHINAS

When outsiders think of the billion people of China, they tend to think of the Han race. True, the people usually regarded as the 'Chinese' make up 94 per cent of the population of the People's Republic of China. But there are at least seventy million non-Han within the sprawling borders. They range from proud and ancient nations like the Mongols and the Manchus to tiny tribes of nomads living on the frigid banks of the Black Dragon River or in the humid misty mountains of Yunnan.

Although the Chinese trace their major race back in antiquity to early cultivators on the banks of the Yellow River, the word Han is a cultural rather than a racial description. Such was the glory of the Han dynasty (206 BC – 220 AD) that ever since the people have proudly described themselves as 'men of Han'. Even within the Han race there are enormous cultural, linguistic and physical differences, just as there are in the 'European' race. The boat people of the southern coast, the Tanka, are racial Han, although their clothing, habits and tongue are very distinctive. The fiery sixty million Cantonese would erupt if anyone suggested they were not of pure Chinese race although they tend to be physically smaller than their cousins of the north and their dialect is a separate language. The Hakka, tough and dour, are scattered not only through China itself but also widely over Southeast Asia. They may be known as the gypsies of China, but would anyone claim that Deng Xiaoping and Lee Kuan Yew were not Chinese, first, last and always?

Outside the diverse and gigantic family of the Han, China today has no fewer than fifty-five registered national minorities. Probably the best known of these are the four million Tibetans whose unique and unlikely culture flowering on the roof of the world has captured imaginations for centuries. But they are outnumbered by other nationalities. In the arid steppes of Xinjiang pro-

The Miao are splintered into many tribes and countless clans, but they all gather in their mountain villages to celebrate the New Year.

vince there are six million Muslim Uygurs – more people than live in Denmark. The Zhuang people, who rule themselves in their own autonomous region of beautiful Guangxi province, number fourteen million, more than the population of the Netherlands. The Dong, the Hani, the Tujia and the Yao are all nations more than a million strong. There are as many people of the Yi race scattered through the southwestern hills as there are Swiss in their native mountains. There are more Hui Muslims in the northwest than the entire population of Saudi Arabia, and in their ancestral homelands, the Mongols and the Manchus hold sway.

Then there are tiny clusters of tribal wanderers like the Ewenki who roam the frozen north, a mere 20 000 of them, whom anthropologists link to the Eskimos of Alaska. Similarly, racial scientists believe the thousand Gaoshan of Taiwan and Fujian are related to the early Polynesians. The Bouyei of Guizhou are pure Thai, the Koreans of Manchuria are directly related to their cousins on the peninsula and the Tartars of Xinjiang are blood brothers to their relatives over the Soviet border in central Asia. In the southwestern provinces nature has been generous indeed with her genes; racial groups trace their bloodlines to a bewildering mixture of Tibetan, Chinese, Thai, Burman, Shan, Karen, Khmer, Polynesian and many other heritages.

How to explain this complexity? Where to begin? Some anthropologists explain there are two Chinas, Inner and Outer. The first, very roughly, lies within the Great Wall and east of Tibet. Here, densely settled and farming intensely, are the Han. About 95 per cent of the population lives in this busy, rich, fertile half of China. In the other half, Outer China – including the far north of Manchuria, the lonely steppes of Mongolia, the ice plateaux of Tibet and Qinghai and the deserts of Xinjiang – live only one in twenty of China's people. The minorities, broadly speaking, live in Outer China. But once again, as with almost everything concerning a nation so complex, so ancient and so diverse as China, generalities are misleading. Today, after four generations of extensive migration, Chinese vastly outnumber Manchus in the northeastern provinces. Similarly, there are many places in Inner China, notably in the amiable racial mixture of Guangxi, Guizhou and Yunnan, where the minorities are very much in the majority.

This baffling but exciting racial melting pot leads to the inevitable question: 'Who is a Chinese?' Is it a person of Han descent or any citizen of the People's Republic? The simple answer is, both. The seventy million people of minority

Arguments still continue among anthropologists as they attempt to trace the origin of the nine minority tribes of the island province of Taiwan.

nationality in China today are as Chinese – and as proud of it – as a Scot is a Briton or a Sioux an American. And just as the Scots preserve their cultural heritage, from tossing the caber to playing the pipes, so do the Zhuang, for example, delight in their spring singing festivals and the Mongols in their wrestling competitions. While benefiting from modern technology, advances in health and education and general improvements in the standard of living, the minorities are keenly proud of their distinctive inheritance in music, drama, poetry, language, dress and religion.

The central government in Beijing jealously preserves the customs, traditions and cultures of the national minorities. They are encouraged, for example, to use their own spoken and written languages alongside the national tongue which all children are taught. Their festivals flourish, their folk customs are subsidised. The minorities are also exempted from some of the responsibilities expected of Han citizens: while Chinese are obliged to strictly adhere to the one-child policy, minority folk can – and enthusiastically do – enjoy large families.

But, protective as it may be towards the sensitivities of the minority nationalities, Beijing is inflexible when it comes to the overall welfare of the people. First, despite official support and encouragement for preserving native languages, every child in the nation must go to school and there must learn Putunghua, commonly known as Mandarin. This applies not only to the minorities, who might speak Turkic, Thai or Tibetan, but also to the scores of millions of Han who speak Chinese dialects like Cantonese, Hakka, Chiu Chow and Fujienese. Some other customs also are now being discouraged. Girls of the Tu nationality of Qinghai were once expected to be safely married off by the age of fifteen; now they have, technically, freedom of choice. Indeed, the women of China, once a second-class minority throughout the land, now enjoy universal protection and laws that guarantee them equal rights. This applies to all women, Han and minorities alike. But customs centuries' old persist despite the law and when a nomadic Kazak girl goes to the altar today she is still carried off after the ceremony, slung over a horse and delivered to the family of her husband-to-be.

Trying to balance the privileges of the minority races with the rights guaranteed to all citizens of the People's Republic is a task that can be both demanding and delicate. The case of the role of women is an example. On the one hand, China promises in its constitution that women are equal and will enjoy

Streetside food vendors in Kunming.

the same status as men; on the other, the rights of the minorities are held to be sacrosanct. So how can Beijing promise women equality while at the same time vowing to preserve the way of life of the nationalities in which millions of Muslim women have traditionally been oppressed? Only by applying commonsense and education. There may be a long way to go, but much progress has been made. This can be seen vividly in the extreme western reaches of the nation where China borders Pakistan. The tribes that straddle the border are identical, their customs of centuries the same, but as travellers now cross the new road that links the two countries, there is a stark and sorry contrast. On the Chinese side, women walk freely and unmasked; as the road rolls down the spectacular passes into Pakistan, women are out of sight in the villages and emerge only in deepest purdah.

If the minorities are pledged rights under the Chinese constitution, they also have responsibilities. Along the troubled border with Vietnam, Zhuang militiamen stand guard alongside regular soldiers of the People's Liberation Army. To the north, Mongols patrol the border of their autonomous region and in Xinjiang, Uygur and Kazak cavalry ride patrol on the long border with Soviet Central Asia.

It is, above all, in the field of education that the Chinese government is striving to improve the standard of living of the seventy million non-Han. Part of this is a conscious effort to compensate for generations of persecution under old regimes, eras in which Muslims in the north and tribes in the southwest were oppressed because of race or religion. Bright minority youngsters are encouraged to further their studies, particularly in fields like agriculture, science, medicine and education. The emphasis of the planners in Beijing is on raising the standard of living, health and knowledge of the national minorities while preserving intact their unique collection of cultures.

Right: Padded against icy blasts from Siberia, a Mongol beats the fierce climate of his homeland.

Overleaf: Drums beat at festive celebrations in southern Guangdong. Photo: Paul Lau.

Above: A game of cards breaks the long hours of lessons.

Right: Faithful to the One God, Muslims in Qinghai province bend in Friday prayer toward Mecca, a continent away.

Overleaf: Through ripening crops in mountain fields, Miao women walk in neat procession. Photo: Paul Lau.

PAUL LAU

*Beside a mud brick house, a young mother of Guangdong, baby strapped
to her back for ease of work in the fields, prepares for another day.*

PAUL LAU

Above: Muslim faithful dominate in a vast swathe of north and west China. Even in Beijing, the Hui can be seen at daily prayers.

Overleaf: Traditional felt tents still dot the steppes where Genghis Khan once rode, giving protection from frigid winds. Photo: Paul Lau.

THE HAN AND THE BARBARIANS

For at least five thousand years, from the dawn of Han civilisation, waves of invaders swept down from the highlands of Tibet and Qinghai, out of the steppes of Mongolia and across the frigid plains of Manchuria to plunder the fabulous riches of China. The Huns came; so did waves of Turkic tribesmen from central Asia; so did the Devil's Horsemen, the dreaded Mongols of the Great Khan.

They came, they admired, they stayed. All left behind a racial legacy which today helps to make up the complex anthropological patchwork map of China's minority nationalities.

But there is a second major historical theme in the racial mix of modern China. As barbarians swept across the Great Wall and into the Han heartland, the Chinese people themselves were on the move. From their native lands inside the huge curl of the Yellow River, over the centuries the Han moved inexorably south. They were propelled by a growing population that needed living space, raw materials for its growing industries and land to till for its increasingly sophisticated agriculture.

As the Han moved south, they came in contact with a bewildering variety of peoples. Many of the tribes and nations moved away ahead of the rising Chinese tide. Others, like numerous branches of the widespread Miao, stayed to live alongside but separate from the newcomers. Others did both; the majority of one group trekked south and west to settle on the fertile plains and become the Thai nation while those who remained are today the colourful 2.2 million Bouyei of the Guizhou mountains.

Relations between the Han and minority tribes were often turbulent and bloody. But the overpowering civilisation of the Han tamed the wild nomad horsemen who came bursting over the Wall and awed the simpler tribesmen

A tribesman in Guizhou clutches his bow, still used today in the hunt for wildlife in the richly forested mountain province.

PAUL LAU

of the south. It happened time and again over the millennia: invaders brandishing swords would swagger into the marble halls of imperial capitals and within a generation, a mere blink of an eye in China's vast sweep of history, their descendants would be truly integrated into the Han culture. It happened when the Mongols ascended the Dragon Throne and proclaimed their dynasty the Yuan. It happened again when the rude Manchus formed the Qing dynasty; they swiftly became more culturally Chinese than the Han themselves. Invaders could come and invaders could go, but the mighty heritage of Han art, culture, cuisine, language, medicine and agriculture absorbed them all.

The obvious benefits of civilisation also impressed the native races that the Chinese confronted as they spread in ever-widening circles to the south and west. As they moved away from their homeland beside the Yellow River, the Han encountered another great waterway, the Yangtse, and settled in its fertile valley. They moved up the river to the rich red earth of the Sichuan basin and down the coast to the paradise provinces of Fujian and Guangdong. As they moved, the original inhabitants either moved in front of them or stayed in place to be assimilated into Chinese culture.

It was not always a peaceful process. Just as settlers in new lands in America, Australia and Africa found violent resistance from those they dispossessed, so did the Han face opposition as they encroached on land traditionally owned by others. The Chinese may have brought with them civilisation, but they were to discover increasingly that many people they encountered had no wish to be civilised and were prompt to do battle with the most urbane of outsiders.

The pattern of southwesterly infiltration, occupation and domination by the Han is one that began more than two thousand years before the Christian era and continued into the present century. It was only after the Second World War that all of Yunnan province came under Beijing's firm grip. First would come explorers, then traders, then soldiers and settlers. When the number of Han increased to a level that threatened the local balance of power, the previous inhabitants had a choice: they could live side by side with the interlopers and share the land; they could assimilate, intermarry and intermingle; they could pack up and seek new homelands for themselves out of reach of the eternal expansion of the Han – or they could fight. The Thais fought, then, overwhelmed, marched off to find new lands. For some time the Viets also moved, before standing to fight for a thousand years along the Gulf of Tonkin.

As the dynasties passed and the Han continued to extend, risings against

Distinctive in its patterns, traditional tribal embroidery is a skill passed from mother to daughter.

29

their rule became both more frequent and more bloody. During the Tang dynasty (618–907 AD) there were 53 major recorded tribal uprisings in Yunnan province. As the Chinese pressed minorities out of Hunan in the age of the Song (960–1279 AD) the native peoples staged 112 wars to save their tribal lands and way of life. During the Ming era (1388–1644 AD) the Zhuang and other tribes of Guangxi rose in revolt 218 times while minorities went to war 91 times in Guizhou and furiously staged 52 wars in Guangdong. But there was no stopping the Han flood.

Ironically, pressure in the south was increased when the Han themselves were conquered from the North by the Manchus in 1644. The new Qing dynasty, although non-Chinese itself, forced waves of Han settlers into the jungles and rich plains of the southwest. For the first time, systematic programs were introduced to detribalise people like the Miao, with bans on their traditional costumes and religious festivals. (At the same time, and for much the same reasons, the English were forcing the Scots to abandon their kilts.) In the eighteenth century, the tribesmen drew their swords. The Miaos of Guizhou fought a full-scale war against Manchu bannermen and Chinese troops in the 1790s. There were ceaseless uprisings by the many minorities of Yunnan; Sichuan was in flames. More seriously, the huge Muslim population of Gansu and Shaanxi declared Holy War. Polynesian and Malay aboriginals on Taiwan, just invaded and occupied by mostly Hakka settlers, fought a stubborn war of resistance. These uprisings were put down with dreadful ferocity; whole tribes were massacred in genocidal revenge. Meanwhile, the Qing dynasty was on the march. Tibet came under the empire, so did Mongolia. Imperial troops marched into the heart of central Asia and added Xinjiang (which means 'new region') to the realm.

It was this military expansion of the Manchu rulers – endless expeditions into wild frontiers coupled with systematic settling of Chinese in tribal lands – that resulted in the racial composition, fortunately now peaceful and friendly, of the country in the twentieth century.

Right: Dressed in tribal finery, a Guizhou belle manages a shy smile for the visitor.

Overleaf: Amid golden rape seed, farmers stand before limestone scarps typical of remote Guizhou. Scattered from here to Laos, Kampuchea and Thailand, Guizhou still holds a majority of the Miao peoples. Photo: Paul Lau.

FAUL LAU

Above: Clutching a goat, a prized highland species, a Dong girl wears embroidered tribal fashion.

Left: Everyone gets splashed with water as Dai peoples of the southwest celebrate the water festival that signals the arrival of the monsoon.

Overleaf: Despite attempts by the central government of China to bring minorities into the mainstream, many prefer the traditional peasant life. Photo: Paul Lau.

PAUL LAU

Above: A Miao festival market in Guizhou province.

Left: Bent under a stack of quick-growing wheat harvested in the brief summer, a Tibetan carries home the crop from his high alpine fields.

Overleaf: Dancers of the Dong minority gather for the Third of March Festival in Fulu, Guangxi province. Photo: Paul Lau.

39

LEONG KA TAI

ON THE PLAINS OF
MANCHURIA

The Manchus today are a small minority within their ancient homeland. For centuries after they stormed south in 1644 to establish the Qing dynasty that ruled China until 1911, the Manchus jealously kept their frozen homeland for themselves. It was not until 1859 that Chinese were allowed to emigrate out of a narrow pale of settlement around the northern shore of the Gulf of Bohai, and the process only really turned from a trickle to a human flood at the dawn of the twentieth century. As soon as the Manchus broke through the Great Wall and installed themselves in power in Beijing, they in turn erected barricades to stop their new subjects heading into the near-empty Manchu homelands. Once the Han broke out of the artificial barriers (they were confined within a wooden stockade whose walls stretched for scores of miles) they burst forth to farm the rich soil and utilise the boundless natural resources. It was a mass migration on the same scale, and only a few decades later, as the American conquest of the west, which was carried out for much the same reasons.

Today, the five million Manchus live mostly in the three northern provinces which together are known in China as 'Dung-bei' or northeast. Almost lost in a sea of seventy million Chinese, they may be accurately called the invisible minority. As many as two million other Manchus may live submerged within the general population, completely integrated and invisible among the Han. Their long occupation of the Dragon Throne helped make the Manchu the most assimilated of the large minority nationalities in China. Widespread intermarriage, especially in the north, means that millions of Han carry some Manchu blood. But racially, as well as culturally, the once-mighty Manchus have been largely absorbed by the Han Chinese they went to conquer.

Modern Manchuria contains traces of other minorities. During the period of Tsarist expansion, Russian engineers constructed railways across Man-

An old Korean in traditional dress, his hat a modern accessory.

43

churia. As white Russians fled Siberia after the 1917 revolution, they helped the European population of Harbin soar; with 200 000 Russians living in the northern city in the 1920s there was good reason for it to be known as the Moscow of Manchuria. Most have since departed – a bare few thousand remain – but distinctive architecture in Harbin and other towns and cities recalls this brief historic chapter.

More permanent are the 1.8 million Koreans living in their own autonomous prefectures, mostly situated close to the borders of North Korea. They started moving into the Manchu lands three centuries ago as the original inhabitants hurried south to grab the plums of newly defeated China. The Koreans remain, and retain much of their own very different culture.

Groups of nomadic Tungusic-speaking tribes, related vaguely far back in history to the Manchus, still roam the frozen forests, hunting, fishing and tending herds as hardy as themselves. Virtually unknown are the Ewenki tribespeople who guide their bark canoes along the northern streams during the sudden summer thaws. The tiny Oroqen tribespeople, a mere four thousand known as the Reindeer Tungus, tend their herds in the bitter far north of Heilongjiang, in whose frigid waters other minorities haul nets for caviar-laden sturgeon. While today the northeast boasts industrial centres like Shenyang, with five million people living beneath its belching smokestacks, much of the region is still rural, and here, small pockets of Manchus retain their traditional lifestyle as herdsmen. But much of the rolling prairies has been transformed into huge wheat farms and, just as in the Canadian wheatlands, huge combine tractors reap the crop that springs up during the brief summer.

Right: Suspicious of strangers, this Korean girl looks askance at a camera.

Overleaf: In autonomous areas close to the Korean border, settlements of Koreans maintain their traditional culture. Photo: Paul Lau.

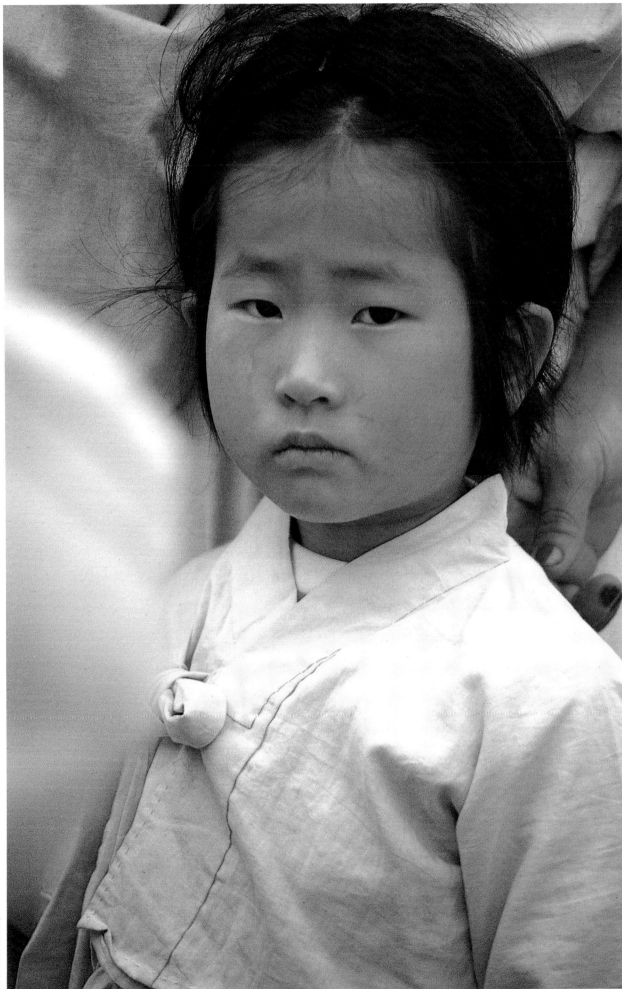

Above: A Korean housewife cleans rice for the family meal.

Right: Mother looks on with critical approval as a Korean girl sews a traditional quilt.

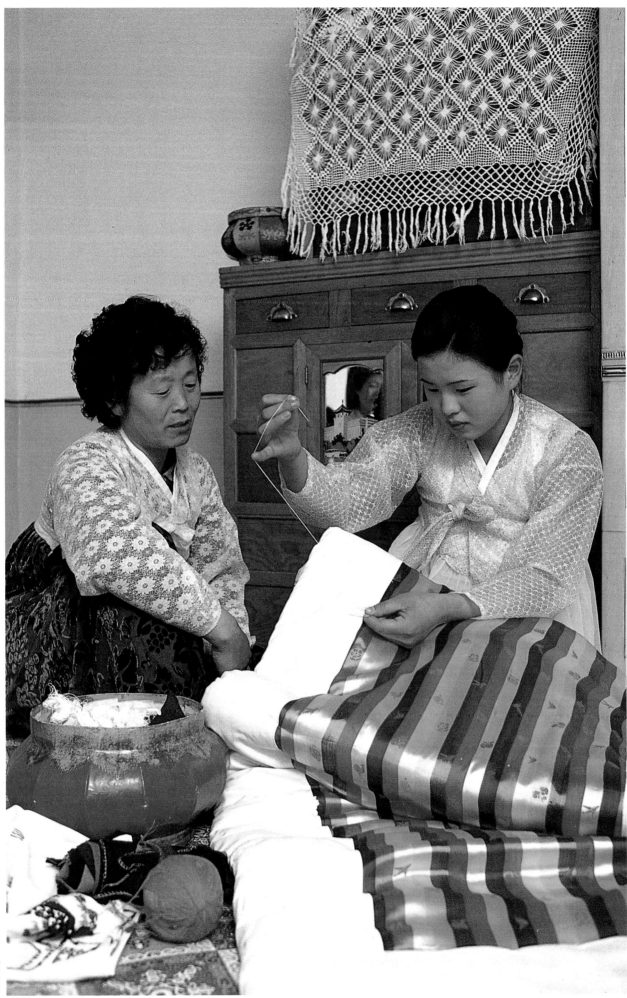

Adorned in her best clothes, this Korean girl is one of a large community of her race who lives in the great Manchurian city of Harbin. On the windowsill, a precious ginseng root, long prized for its medicinal purposes, gives its beneficial additives to a bottle of vodka.

PAUL LAU

Above: Drums ready to sound the start of celebrations, young musicians await a signal to begin.

Overleaf: Koreans live close to the floor for good reason. Fires under the flooring provide the only source of heat and in the bitter cold it is wise to get as close to it as possible. Photo: Paul Lau.

THE MONGOLIAN GRASSLANDS

Until the thirteenth century, nobody outside the lonely plains of north Asia had heard of a warring, wandering tribe called the Mongols. Since then, nobody has forgotten them. The ruthless ferocity of the Devil's Horsemen, led by their brutal but brilliant young chieftain, Temujin, exploded the Mongols from obscurity to the very centre of the world stage. Genghis Khan, as he has gone down in history, galloped at the head of his Golden Horde across half the world, forging the largest land empire in history. His grandson, the Great Kublai, ruled China; under the Yuan dynasty his empire was extended greatly.

It is difficult today to picture the friendly, hospitable 2.5 million Mongols of China as the dreaded conquerers in front of whom the world bowed in terror. Visitors to their round felt tents are bade welcome, given a potation of virile fermented mare's milk and invited to sprawl on the rugs and cushions that serve as furniture. Outside on the endless grasslands that sweep across northern China like a 2000 kilometre-long scimitar, the pride of the Mongols graze. Even seven centuries after the death of Temujin, the horse remains the greatest glory of the plainsman. Like their owners, the Mongol ponies tend to be stocky, strong and enduring.

The Mongols today are scattered across the world they once ruled. They can be found in small enclaves in European Russia; other tiny communities exist as far away as distant Yunnan, remnant of a frontier garrison never recalled when the Yuan dynasty crumbled. But most Mongols live within the autonomous region where they outnumber two to one the population of the bordering independent country of Outer Mongolia.

Under a policy of encouraging settled agriculture, many Mongols now live in brick houses instead of the traditional *yer*. But no matter where they live, traditions remain. One of these is wrestling, the national sport and a discipline that relies more on skill and speed than brute strength. Their other great love

Dressed in festive best, a family group poses nervously in a nomad tent pitched on the endless Mongol steppe.

55

is riding and across the 1.1 million square kilometre vast swathe that is the Inner Mongolian Autonomous Region horsemen young and old ceaselessly gallop over the endless horizons. Both activities call for long and thirsty post-mortems. But making *airag* from the milk of their horses is a complicated and tedious process and the modern visitor is more likely to be offered beer or Chinese rice spirit as a drink over which to discuss the relative merits of man or beast.

Centuries ago, the Mongols enthusiastically embraced the teachings of Buddhism. Some say they were converted by wandering monks, others suggest that soldiers picked up the faith while garrisoned in Tibetan communities. Whatever the cause, in many families the oldest son was traditionally consigned for life to a lamasery. Many of the temples were destroyed or converted for other uses during the Cultural Revolutionary drive against religion, but in recent years, under more liberal rule, they have reopened and young Mongols are again free to take on the robes of the religious; a significant number do so.

The centre of Mongol life, however, remains the open horizons of the grasslands. They remain first and foremost herdsmen and despite efforts to encourage communal farming techniques the Mongols, more than most people in modern China, have managed to remain independently aloof. With their horses, camels, sheep, cattle and yaks, they are to a large degree free to roam in search of forage for their animals. As the Mongol family moves over the plains with its heavy felt tent bundled into a cart pulled by oxen or camel, the young men whip their horses into a gallop. With rifles across their backs, swaying sideways in the saddle as they pursue a fleeing fox or other game, it is easy to glimpse how this formidable people rode to glory with the Great Khan.

Right: Scattered far into China, small enclaves of Mongols exist far from the homeland, like this man of Henan province.

Overleaf: The horizon limitless under the big skies of the steppes, the grasslands of Mongolia roll away to infinity. Photo: Paul Lau.

PAUL LAU

*Above: The warm high-crowned fur hats of the plains are worn for prac-
tical as well as fashionable reasons.*

*Left: Even in the towns, many people still prefer the spacious snugness of
a felt tent instead of a modern apartment.*

Above: Carrying home kindling wood through the warm tropical mist of a Guangdong morning.

Right: Warm clothes are needed to ward off the icy blasts that sweep the treeless plains of the Mongol homeland.

Overleaf: For half the year, the steppes are hot and dry. For the rest, the ground is frozen solid. Photo: Paul Lau.

PEOPLE OF THE STEPPES

They used to call it the Road of the Emperor when it connected the glorious court of the Han dynasty to a dimly rumoured barbarian kingdom named Rome, far to the uncivilised west. Then it was known as the Jade Road and the Fur Road. Only a century ago, three hundred years after the main camel caravans had ceased plodding along its treacherous, deadly route, did it become known as the Silk Road. Along the ancient paths of trade came many peoples. There were bandits and brigands, herdsmen and galloping nomads, in addition to imperial garrisons and adventurous merchants. Many of them from both east and west stayed to colonise the steppes, deserts and oases of Central Asia. Today, their descendants remain, making up communities that comprise the most obvious non-Chinese racial groups in China.

Xinjiang means 'New Region' because it came back under the Imperial fold only last century. But it had been Chinese two thousand years before, then an area of chaos, then Chinese again, then the haunt of nomadic bandits, then a target for both British and Russian expansionism as the rival nations fought in Central Asia. Teachers came as well as traders and ideas penetrated China along with gold to pay for silk. Christianity, Buddhism, Zoroastrianism were all ideas that travelled on the lonely road before the torrent of Islam swept all before it. These tides of beliefs and settlers left behind a rich tapestry of races in Xinjiang.

The dominant race on the steppes are the Turkic Uygur people, six million of them, whose eyes tell of their non-Han ethnic extraction. They are the most numerous of the sixteen minorities, mostly Muslims, who share the vast arid plains, the fertile valleys and oases, the beautiful pastures and the arid hills of Xingjiang, Ningxia, Gansu and Qinghai. The Uygurs' racial heritage is obviously Caucasian. Many of them look like Greeks. Their language is close to Turkish but written in Arabic script. The Uygurs are proud of their distinctive

Split by boundaries carved through the open plains and sands of central Asia, the Uygur of China's Xinjiang province are racial brothers of the people of Turkestan over the Soviet border.

culture and in the grape-growing oases around their capital of Urumqi artisans beat silver, fashion their own musical instruments, dance traditional steps and pray in mosques considered as beautiful as any in the Islamic world.

In most of the towns and cities, from Lanzhou, the ancient frontier town in the poverty province of Gansu, right out to Kashqar on the fringe of Soviet Central Asia, the most prominent buildings are the mosques. For here runs the writ of Islam and not only are ethnic minorities like Uygurs, Uzbeks, Tartars, Sala and Xibo devout followers of the Prophet but many Han have been converted over the centuries and make up the Hui, China's most numerous religious minority outside the broad Buddhist-Confucian-Taoist mainstream. Beijing recognises the Hui as a distinct national minority, 7.5 million strong. The Ningxia Autonomous Region is the official homeland for the Hui, but numerically more of them live in neighbouring Gansu. A century ago, the Hui rose against imperial rule and expeditionary forces put down their revolt with appalling savagery; the death toll was in the millions. Today, most Hui are racially indistinguishable from Han and their language is identical to the other Chinese among whom they live. Only the strictures of their religion – circumcision, regular prayers and avoidance of pork – tell the Hui apart from the Han.

In the streets of cities like Urumqi and Kashqar, the smells and spices of kebabs grilling on streets, the wail of Tajik horns, all bring to mind the culture of the Middle East. Across the plains proud Kirghir horsemen display their skills. Over the border, their cousins are called Cossacks and the million of them whose tents dot the grasslands of the steppes of China are no less fearsome when aroused than the legendary warriors of Russia.

Indeed, the steppes are peopled by races who, until a few years ago, paid little heed to borders. Mongols, Kazaks, Uzbeks, Tibetans still roam across huge swathes of Qinghai grassland, Xinjiang desert and sparse plains of Gansu. Others stay put in the ancient trading towns that were the staging posts for caravans that carried Marco Polo and other adventurers along the Silk Road.

In recent years, industrialisation has brought a wave of Han migration to areas that were once peopled mainly by minorities, and the Uygurs are now a minority in their own autonomous region.

Right: A rickety donkey cart, coaxed on by a local Turpan man.

Overleaf: Tianchi, the Lake of Heaven, in Xinjiang.
Photo: Mike Langford/Horizon.

Above: Proud mother urges a reluctant smile from a son unused to strangers.

Right: The colourful interior of a yurt tent.

72

JAN WHITING SUBIACO

Above: Famed for 2000 years for its grapes, the oasis of the Turpan basin provides the most famed melons in China and grapes that press into juicy wines.

Left: The old of the Arabic religious script and the turban of Islam mix with the electronic age of the microphone being used to spread the Word of God in this Hui mosque in Harbin.

Overleaf: A young Uramgi mother and daughter. Photo: Mike Langford/Horizon.

MIKE LANGFORD/HORIZON

Above: In the harsh climate of Tibet, Tibetans clutch to family ties and hold to their own unique brand of Buddhism.

Left: In Xinjiang, ancestral homeland of the Turks, this Uygur girl from Turpan shows features and clothes that would not be out of place in Istanbul.

Overleaf: A whisper of Arabia penetrates this mosque in Beijing where prayers are offered for the dead. Photo: Paul Lau.

THE TIBETAN
SHANGRI-LA

Nobody knows from where the Tibetans came. For many centuries the Chinese empire was well aware of the fierce, feuding kingdoms in the rugged mountains beyond the fringes of civilisation. Bands of plundering horsemen periodically swept down to ravage outposts of Han settlement, but it was not until the seventh century that close bonds were formed between the two societies. Then, the Tibetan king Songtsen Gampo married the beautiful Tang princess, Wen Chen. She took with her into the alpine vastnesses more than a rich dowry; she is also credited with helping introduce the Buddhist faith into the region.

Today it is hard to imagine Tibet without its unique form of the Buddhist religion. To a greater extent than any other nationality in China, the Tibetans live their faith. It is a part of every waking moment, and even as a nomad herdsman cuts the throat of a sheep that provides his basic diet, he utters prayers for forgiveness.

The trappings of Mahayana Buddhism — the red gowns of the lamas, the eerie moan from the three-metre horns echoing down the valleys, the splendour of the Potala Palace rising fortress-like above Lhasa — have long created a vivid picture of the Tibetan way of life that has captured the imagination of millions. But behind this Shangri-La facade of happy herdsmen poking out their tongues in polite greeting and devout monks ceaselessly counting their rosaries there lay a more unpleasant reality. In the feudal past that ended only a few decades ago, most Tibetan peasants led brutish, often short lives. More often than not they were serfs chained in grim servitude to either aristocratic or monastic landlords. Up to half the male population was in the lamaseries, thus putting an immense workload on the rest of the population. The land was riddled with bandits, disease, superstition and want.

Few societies in China suffered as dreadfully in the mindless fury of the

Once banned, still discouraged, religion never faded in the hearts of Tibetans. Today, in more relaxed times, young men once again can turn to the monasteries for a contemplative life.

83

great proletarian Cultural Revolution as the lamas of Tibet. But for the hardy folk who inhabit the treeless, stony ice plateau on the roof of the world, religion is woven firmly into the fabric of their being. Two decades after the Red Guards rampaged through the monasteries, destroying precious relics of the Tibetans' much-loved Buddhist faith, temples throughout the country are rising again, the prayer wheels spin in every village and on countless spurs and hillsides throughout the vastness of the high land, flags bearing Buddhist scriptures flutter in the eternal winds.

Today, life for the four million Tibetans contains more than *chos*, as they call their faith. After the failed uprising against Chinese rule was put down in 1959, a wave of organised Han settlement rolled into the bleak but beautiful plateau. Many of the thousands of lamaseries were closed down, the monks and nuns put to work. Distasteful as these tactics may have been to many Tibetans, none can deny that the increased Chinese presence has meant better medical care, vastly improved education, eradication of illiteracy and leprosy, huge strides in agriculture and a general improvement in the standard of living in the towns. For the half of the Tibetan people that roams the 1 210 000 square kilometres of Tibet itself, and spreads far across the high country of Qinghai, Sichuan, Yunnan and Gansu, the Chinese presence in Lhasa has not made much difference to a way of life that has remained basically unchanged for a thousand years.

Despite the improvements in material existence, Tibetans are keenly aware that something is missing from their spiritual lives. They yearn for the return over the Himalayas of the Dalai Lama, the fourteenth 'living Buddha' who fled to political asylum in India in 1959.

Right: A quizzical Kampa, his woven turban identifying his highland clan, looks toward an uncertain future.

Overleaf: High in the Tibetan mountains, yaks are the only form of transport. Photo: Geoff Bartram/Horizon.

Fierce Kampa tribesmen waged a fifteen-year civil war against Chinese occupation of Tibet. Today, the Kampa cling determinedly to their Buddhist faith and pray for the return of the exiled Dalai Lama.

JAN WHITING SUBIACO

A winning smile for strangers gives welcome to a Tibetan town. Famed for hospitality, the Tibetan method of welcome is to stick out the tongue.

Above: Shielded from highland sun by a light umbrella, for most of the year Tibetans need more effective protection from the extremes of their harsh climate.

Right: A colourful mixture of old and new garments adorn this couple in Lhasa.

Overleaf: Guangze women in a field of wildflowers. Photo: Mike Langford/Horizon.

THE MOUNTAIN
MELTING POT

Nowhere in China is there such a vibrant racial mixture as in the exotic mountain provinces of the southwest. Through the jumbled terrain of Guizhou across the ranges of Yunnan and in the pleasant valleys of Guangxi live a startling selection of peoples. They are an ethnic heritage left behind by history; a confusion of differing strains who these days live together in harmony. It was not always so. As the Han pressed out of the confines of China proper, waves of other peoples retreated before them. There was warfare, whole peoples were enslaved, some obliterated, as the Han tide extended. Under Mongol and Manchu dynasties, the process continued. But it was a slow development; indeed, parts of Yunnan did not come under effective sway of the government in far distant Beijing until after liberation in 1949.

Terrible as were the excesses of the past, they have resulted in a modern wonderland for the amateur anthropologist. To wander the hills of the southwest is to venture into an area of rare fascination. The land, with its limestone scarps and granite outcrops, provides a graphic background for the picturesque people of two-score nationalities.

If they seem continually at play, that is because each different minority group celebrates its own festivals, folksong gatherings and tribal religious holidays. In Guizhou, where seven million minority people make up more than a quarter of the population, there are over one hundred major festivals and thousands of minor ones celebrated every year. In one such festival, travellers can see colourfully dressed Bouyei tribespeople throwing water over strangers. It should come as no surprise that this is an identical practice to festivities which take place in Thailand: the Bouyei are the Thais who stayed behind in China when the rest of what became the Thai nation fled from suppression one thousand years ago.

Pockets remain of a lifestyle unchanged for centuries. This Yao farmwife is off to the fields to till in the same way as her great-grandmother coaxed a living from the good earth of Guangdong.

Remote, until recent times largely unknown, Guizhou is almost custom-built to provide a strikingly photogenic background for tribal peoples. Geography has furnished a confused landscape with huge outcrops of granite and sandstone broken by rivers. Roads were unknown until recent years. Amid this jumble of high ranges cut by ravines, different communities have flourished, cut off not only from the outside world but from each other. On the peak of unlikely escarpments that look like the pattern for traditional Chinese paintings, perch Miao villages. Down by the riverside live the Bouyei. In Guizhou there are more Miao than anywhere else on earth. About three million strong, they are subdivided into a bewilderment of tribes, like the Flower Miao who, long before the hippies, were wearing flowers in their hair.

Other Guizhou festivals are distinctively local affairs, like the bullfights of the Dong. Every village raises its Dong bull, bred for strength to pull the wooden ploughs through the heavy mud of paddyfields, and endurance to defeat rival bulls from neighbouring villages. During harvest festivals, drum-beating, gong-clanging processions of villagers escort their huge local champion water buffaloes to nearby natural amphitheatres in the hills. As the bulls lock horns and clash and strain to topple each other, the Dong cheer on their favourite beasts and toast them in fiery mao tai. Visitors to all festivals are welcomed enthusiastically.

Guangxi has traditionally had such a high percentage of Zhuang people that, officially, the entire province is a self-governing autonomous region with the governor and deputy governor usually coming from the thirteen million-strong nationality. Zhuang make up fully a third of Guangxi's population.

After centuries of cohabitation, especially with their Cantonese-speaking neighbours, the Zhuang are now mostly indistinguishable from Han. But they proudly keep their own traditions, some of which are unique – such as the spring songfests in which young men and women stand beneath groves of towering yellow-stemmed bamboo and chorus songs of love to potential marriage partners. When the summer monsoon starts to sigh over the Gulf of Tonkin and onto the green slopes of Guangxi, the hills and valleys are truly alive with the sound of music.

Yunnan has well over twenty nationalities, some of them, like the Bai, Hani and Miao, numbering more than a million. But in every mountain valley there seems to be a settlement of some obscure, small tribal group. There are the colourful Bulang, the evasive Dulong, who number but four thousand, the

Notched together without nails, Dong carpentry is a victory of native architecture.

smiling Achang, the Nu – the list is almost endless. On every hilltop there seem to be Miao outposts, often lovely villages affording challenging vistas over unsurpassed, unspoiled ranges.

All these delightful minorities have their own distinctive colourful tribal fashions: the elaborate silver hairpieces and heavy jewellery of Miao girls often comprise the wealth of their villages. And there are regional culinary delights throughout the mountains – freshwater turtle stewed in its own shell, anteater with garlic – that make a visit into the tribal highlands as memorable to the palate as to the eyes.

Above: Under a festive scarf, a Dong tribesman observes a village rite.

Right: Dong men claim that their womenfolk are the most beautiful of all the many hill tribes of Guangxi province.

Overleaf: Rival villages train their buffaloes in combat and entire villages will walk for many kilometres to cheer on their champions in annual New Year bouts. Photo: Paul Lau.

PAUL LAU

Above: In elaborate traditional costume, this girl of the She minority from the Southeast is dressed for her wedding day.

Left: Boasting dark glasses and a stainless steel watch, this young novice is waiting to help bless a new house in Guizhou.

Overleaf: China's largest minority race, the Zhuang, are among the most skilled farmers in the nation. Photo: Paul Lau.

LEONG KA TAI

Above: Their bright robes glowing, young Dai boys take a break from seminary studies.

Right: Framed by timbered walls of their home in the hills, these young Bouyei people are the Thais who stayed behind.

Overleaf: The Black Hat subtribe of the Miao people are easily identified by their unique garb. Photo: Paul Lau.

106

WHAT FUTURE IN A HAN SEA?

What is a Chinese? Who is Chinese? There are complex answers to these seemingly simple questions. In the official viewpoint of Beijing, a Chinese is any citizen of the People's Republic of China. But without doubt, the people of Hong Kong, Taiwan, the twenty million overseas Chinese of Southeast Asia and the people in Chinatowns all over the world are also Chinese. But are the seventy million non-Han inside China 'Chinese'? By nationality, certainly. By race, often – as in the case of the Hui whose only distinction is usually their religion. By persuasion, occasionally – as in Tibet, where rule from Beijing is still largely a matter of imposed power. By assimilation, very widely, as evidenced by the integration of Mongol and Manchu who came to China to conquer and remained to be civilised.

So how, today, do the great mass of Chinese, the Han, regard the minority nationalities with whom they share fully half the vast country? By and large, the tribal, racial and religious minorities are subject to a policy of benign positive discrimination. They are given favourable official treatment in many ways, some of which make the minorities the envy of their Han neighbours.

One of the most obvious aspects of this is the large presence in national policy-making bodies of minority representatives. In the National Peoples Consultative Council, there are several places reserved for delegates from autonomous regions and minority areas. On a per capita ratio this gives them twice the number of seats to which they would be entitled on a simple percentage basis. Of course, these delegates are all loyal Party or government officials who are not going to rock the ship of state, but, nevertheless, they are a powerful symbol of the non-Han minority and a positive statement of the importance Beijing places on the nationalities. It would be foolish and naive to claim that there was no discrimination or differences between the diverse racial and religi-

Tibetans stray far from their icy homeland and this woman in the Sichuan hills is from a Tibetan community which has for centuries farmed the lands under the clouds.

111

ous groups in China today. Of course, there is. But the official policy is that all groups have the right to expect respect for their way of life and beliefs inside the greater whole of a socialist way of life.

In day-to-day life, the minorities largely rule themselves. The five autonomous regions (Tibet, Mongolia, Ningxia, Guangxi and Xinjiang) have the same political status and government structures as the provinces themselves. Indeed, in the case of the Guangxi Zhuang Autonomous Region, the Zhuang hold the political reins of power in a vital border province in which they are now outnumbered by Hans. Uygurs rule Uygurs in Xinjiang. Mongols govern Mongolia and Tibetans are increasingly being educated and encouraged to take charge of their land. Overall, of course, the national interest takes precedence and those minority politicians in the provinces are loyal communist functionaries. Within the broader demands of state policy, however, they efficiently represent their own unique constituencies.

Throughout China, inside provincial boundaries, there is a patchwork quilt of political units. The aim is wherever possible to have people governed by their own kind. To this end, there are thirty autonomous prefectures; some of them huge areas larger than European nations, others containing populations of hundreds of thousands. There are seventy-five autonomous counties where local government is in the hands of local people.

In these racial enclaves, folk festivals, culture, traditions, architecture, crafts, song, sports, cuisine, literature and legends of the minorities are not only preserved but actively encouraged by both the central government in Beijing and by provincial governments. Even during the lunacy of the Cultural Revolution when Red Guards ran riot and persecuted and dragged down the most powerful in the land, there was a hands-off policy that gave some measure of protection to racial and religious minority groups. The Hui, for example, were largely exempt from the worst excesses of the Red Guards, in vivid contrast to the horrific treatment meted out to Christians and the barbaric destruction of some of the most ancient Buddhist temples.

Today, development of the minority areas follows broadly the economic and social policies aimed at making China a modern and prosperous nation by the next century. The Four Modernisations of agriculture, industry, defence and science and technology are stressed in autonomous regions and self-governing prefectures in the same manner as they are in the rest of the nation. The national leadership in Beijing has made it plain that while cultural diversity

A triumph of modern China is that the people of many differing tribes, faiths and backgrounds can live together in harmony.

and racial traditions are to be allowed to thrive, they will not be permitted to flourish at the cost of backwardness and poverty. Great stress is laid on the education of the minorities' children with advanced technical, medical and agricultural higher education built on a framework of compulsory basic learning in the national tongue, Putunghua. In every corner of the land, children are now fluent in Mandarin in addition to the language or dialect they speak at home. For the first time in history, Miao and Mongol, Uygur and Hui, Korean and Kazak can talk to each other and to Han Chinese in a common language. This universal grasp of a common tongue has united the disparate peoples that comprise modern China. It has provided a basis on which all can work together for the common good of the races that make up the People's Republic of China.

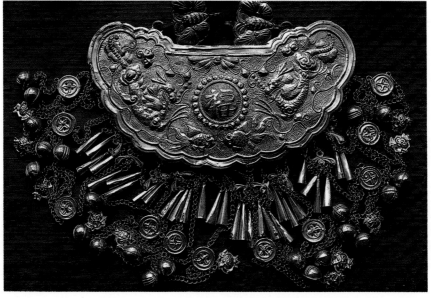

PAUL LAU

Above: For many of the hill peoples of the southwest, the family heirlooms are the riches of the clan.

Right: A street vendor displays his wares.

Overleaf: Harvest time in the rich ricefields of Guangdong.
Photo: Paul Lau.

JAN WHITING SUBIACO

Above: This young scholar in Harbin knows well that the future of all China lies in education.

Left: Four faces of modern China.

Above: Village industries abound, old skills still triumph, in many a rural Chinese community. This Uygur blacksmith hammers out steel from his private forge.

Right: China's new economic policies that allow farmers to sell their excess goods — and pocket the profits — have seen a doubling of rural output and have made the peasants of China wealthier that at any time in their long history.

Overleaf: Terraced over the years at enormous cost in human toil, the steep hillsides provide fertile farmland. Photo: Paul Lau.

DISTRIBUTION AND POPULATION OF MINORITY NATIONALITIES

Nationality	Population	Area
Achang	20 000	Yunnan
Bai	1.2 million	Yunnan
Baoan	9000	Gansu
Benglong	10 000	Yunnan
Bouyei	2.2 million	Guizhou
Bulang	58 000	Yunnan
Dai	839 000	Yunnan
Daur	94 000	Inner Mongolia, Heilongjiang, Xinjiang
Dong	1.5 million	Guizhou, Hunan, Guangxi
Dongxiang	279 000	Gansu, Xinjiang
Dulong	4000	Yunnan
Ewenki	19 000	Inner Mongolia, Heilongjiang
Gaoshan	1000	Taiwan, Fujian
Gelao	53 000	Guizhou, Guangxi, Sichuan, Hunan
Hani	1 million	Yunnan
Hezhe	1400	Heilongjiang
Hui	7.5 million	Ningxia, Gansu
Jing	10 000	Guangxi
Jingpo	93 000	Yunnan
Jinuo	10 000	Yunnan
Kazak	907 000	Xinjiang, Gansu, Qinghai
Kirghir	113 000	Xinjiang, Heilongjiang
Korean	1.8 million	Jilin, Heilongjiang, Inner Mongolia
Lahu	300 000	Yunnan
Li	810 000	Guangdong
Lisu	480 000	Yunnan, Sichuan
Luoba	2000	Tibet
Manchu	4.5 million	Liaoning, Jilin, Heilongjiang, Hebei, Reijung, Inner Mongolia
Maonan	38 000	Guangxi
Menba	6000	Tibet
Miao	5 million	Guizhou, Yunnan, Xinjiang, Liaoning
Mongol	2.5 million	Inner Mongolia, Xinjiang, Liaoning
Mulao	90 000	Guangxi
Naxi	240 000	Yunnan, Sichuan
Nu	23 000	Yunnan
Oroqen	4000	Inner Mongolia, Heilongjiang
Pumi	24 000	Yunnan
Quang	102 000	Sichuan
Russian	2900	Xinjiang
Sala	69 000	Qinghai, Gansu
She	36 000	Fujian, Zhejiang
Shui	280 000	Jiangxi, Guangdong, Guizhou, Guangxi
Tajik	26 000	Xinjiang
Tartar	4000	Xinjiang
Tibetan	4 million	Tibet, Qinghai, Sichuan, Gansu, Yunnan
Tu	150 000	Qinghai, Gansu
Tujia	3 million	Hunan, Hubei, Sichuan
Uygur	6 million	Xinjiang
Uzbek	12 000	Xinjiang
Wa	290 000	Yunnan
Xibo	83 000	Xinjiang, Liaoning, Jilin
Yao	1.5 million	Guangxi, Hunan, Yunnan, Guangdong, Guizhou
Yi	5.5 million	Sichuan, Yunnan, Guizhou, Guangxi
Yugur	10 000	Gansu
Zhuang	14 million	Guangxi, Yunnan, Guangdong, Guizhou

With the stolid endurance of his race, a Korean farmer begins another day.

INDEX

Numbers in italics indicate references to photograph captions.